J   Seuling, Barbara.
621.31
SEU   Flick a switch : how
            electricity gets to
            your home

AR Level: 4.1
DATE DUE   Pts: 0.5

38077

FLICK a SWITCH

HOW *Electricity* GETS TO YOUR HOME

by Barbara Seuling illustrated by Nancy Tobin

HOLIDAY HOUSE / NEW YORK

For Jessie Kristian Nelson
B. S.

To Matthew, Sadie, and Lily
N. T.

www.holidayhouse.com
First Edition

Library of Congress Cataloging-in-Publication Data
Seuling, Barbara.
Flick a switch: how electricity gets to your home / by Barbara Seuling;
illustrated by Nancy Tobin.—1st ed.
p. cm.
Summary: Describes how electricity was discovered, how early devices were invented to make
use of it, how it is generated in power plants and then distributed for many different uses.
ISBN 0-8234-1729-8
1. Electric power—Juvenile literature. 2. Electricity—Juvenile literature. [1.Electricity. 2. Electric
power.] I. Tobin, Nancy, ill. II. Title
TK148.S48 2003
621.31—dc21   2002017143

It's getting dark.
You flick a switch. The room lights up.
Electricity made it happen! But how?
Where did the electricity come from?
How did it get into your house?

Nobody invented electricity. It has always been here.
It was here when the earth began.
It was here in the time of the dinosaurs.
It was here when people came along.
But it took a long time for people to discover it.

There are little bits of electric power in everything.
These little bits are called electrons. Some are in the air.
Some are in rocks. There are even some in you.

Sometimes your hair stands up when you brush it. That's the electricity in your hair being stirred up. It is called static electricity. Static electricity can't make your computer run, but it can do funny things!

Static electricity stays in one place.

Yeah, but I don't!

Static electricity was discovered in ancient Greece when a mathematician named Thales polished some amber with a piece of wool or fur. When he stopped rubbing, bits of feather and straw flew to the stone and stuck there.

Even after people knew there was electricity,
they didn't know how to use it.
They worked heavy machines by hand to do many jobs.
They made their clothes with needles and thread.
They used fire to light their homes and cook their food.

But over the years, people experimented with electricity.
They wanted to find ways to use it.
In 1752, Benjamin Franklin proved that lightning was
a form of electricity. He flew a kite on a stormy day
and held onto the kite string with an iron key attached to it.
When lightning flashed, electricity traveled along the
wet kite string through the metal key and zapped him.

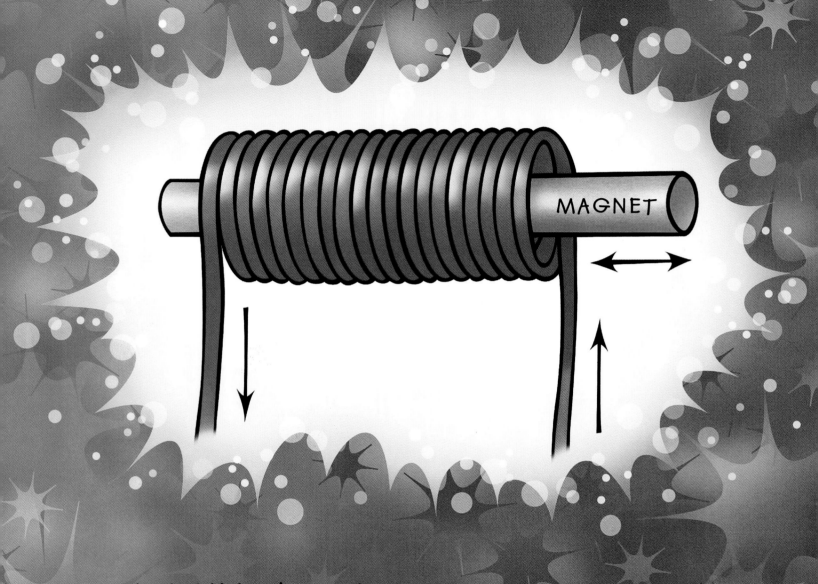

In 1831, Michael Faraday put a magnet inside a coil of
copper wire. Then he moved the magnet back and forth.
The magnet stirred up electrons.
Electric current flowed through the wire.
That was the first generator. The more a generator
turns, the more electric power is produced.
Faraday found a safe way to make electricity.

Batteries, or electric cells, were invented by Alessandro Volta in 1800. We use them now to make toys and flashlights and portable CD players work. Some are even big enough to start car engines. But it takes a power plant to generate enough electricity for a village, a town, or a big city.

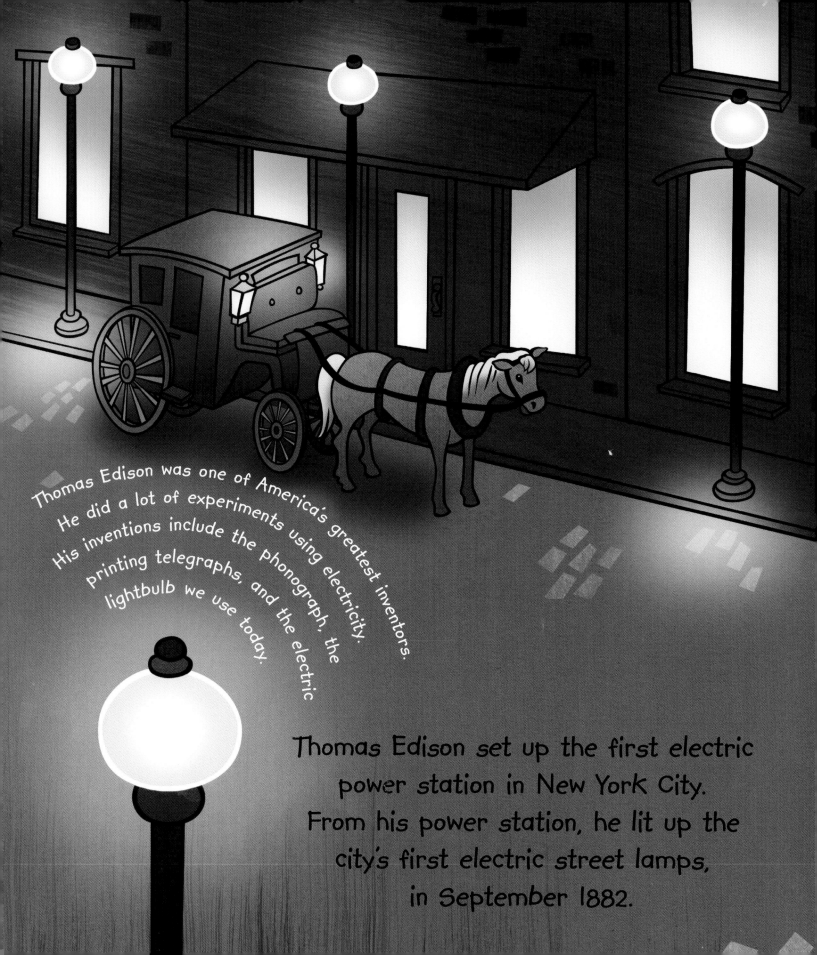

Thomas Edison was one of America's greatest inventors. He did a lot of experiments using electricity. His inventions include the phonograph, the printing telegraphs, and the electric lightbulb we use today.

Thomas Edison set up the first electric power station in New York City. From his power station, he lit up the city's first electric street lamps, in September 1882.

Inside a power plant, a generator turns.
A large magnet inside stirs up electrons.
The generator must keep spinning to produce electricity.
A turbine, a large wheel with blades,
keeps the generator turning.

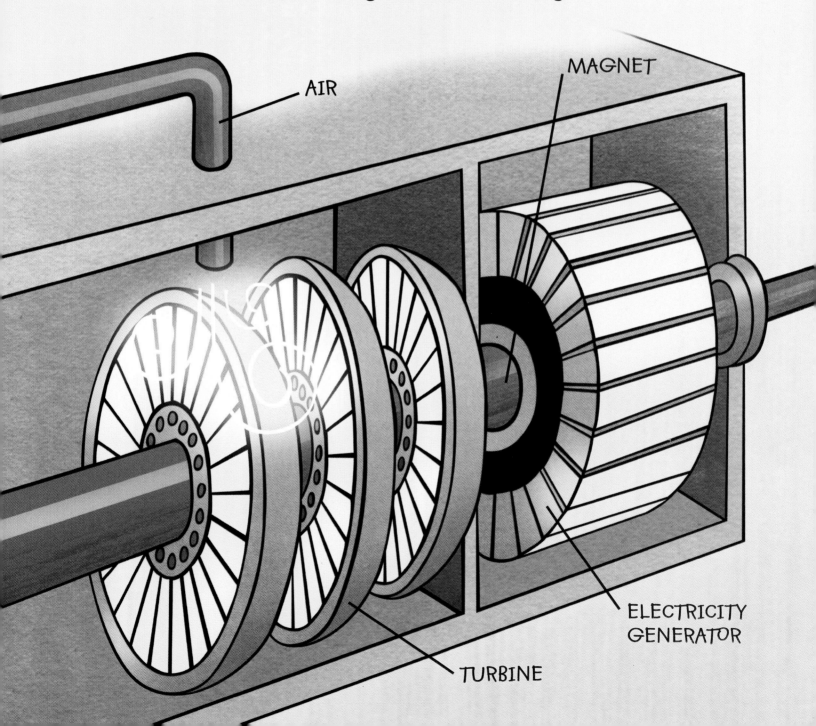

AIR

MAGNET

ELECTRICITY
GENERATOR

TURBINE

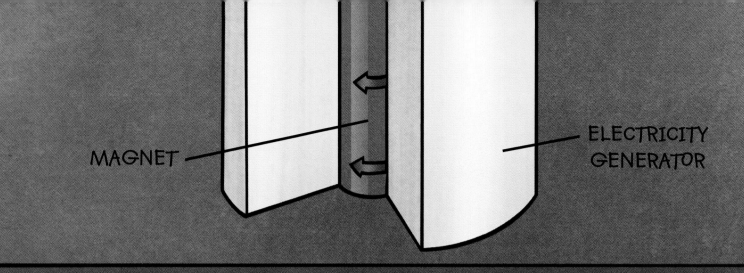

MAGNET

ELECTRICITY GENERATOR

TURBINE

WATER FROM DAM

Many power plants use water to turn the blades
of their turbines. Water comes through a pipe and pushes
the blades. As the blades turn, the generator spins.

Power plants that use water to work their turbines are called hydroelectric plants. (*Hydro* comes from the Greek word for "water.") Other plants use steam, wind, nuclear power, fossil fuels such as coal or gas, or even the sun (solar power) to make their turbines spin.

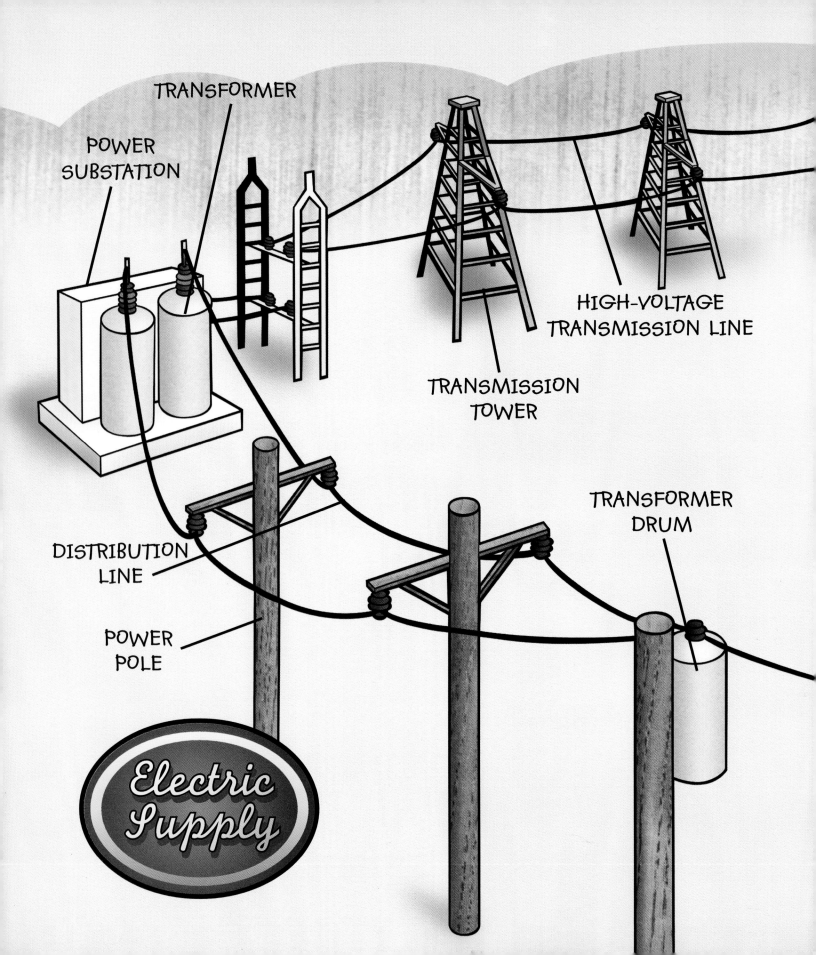

POWER
SUBSTATION

TRANSFORMER

TRANSFORMER

HIGH-VOLTAGE
TRANSMISSION LINE

TRANSMISSION
TOWER

TRANSFORMER
DRUM

DISTRIBUTION
LINE

POWER
POLE

Electric
Supply

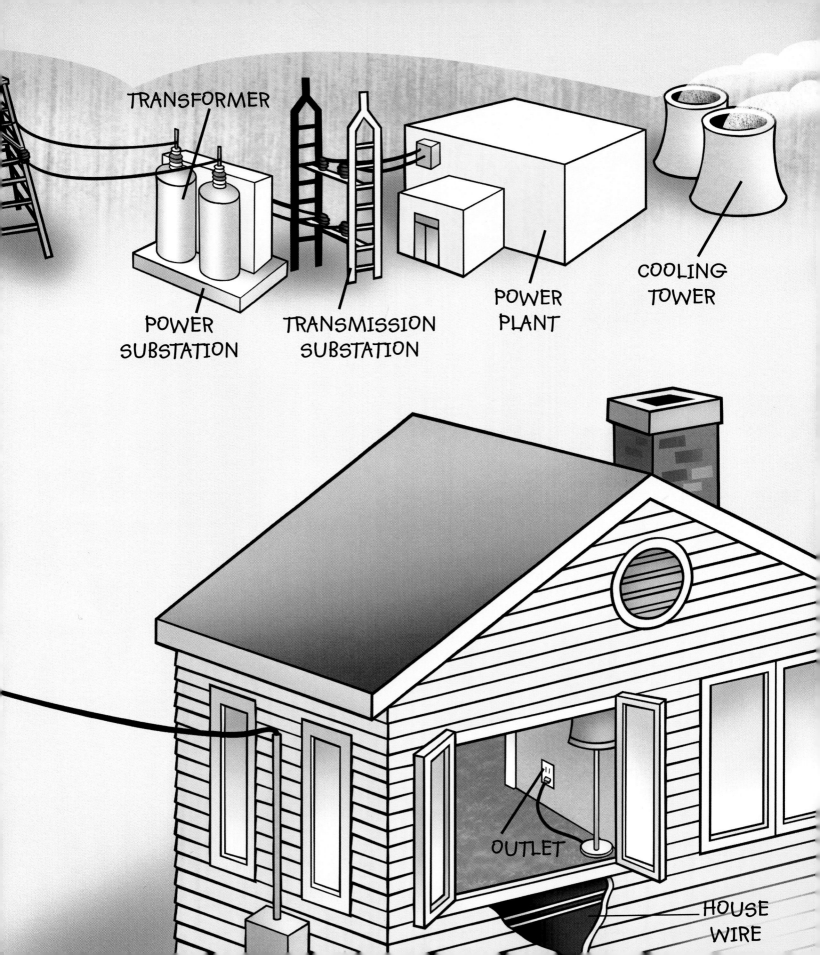

TRANSFORMER

POWER
SUBSTATION

TRANSMISSION
SUBSTATION

POWER
PLANT

COOLING
TOWER

OUTLET

HOUSE
WIRE

Electric power is sent
from a power plant to your
town along metal wires.
Electric power that is moved on
wires is called electric current.
It is easy for electrons
to move along metal.

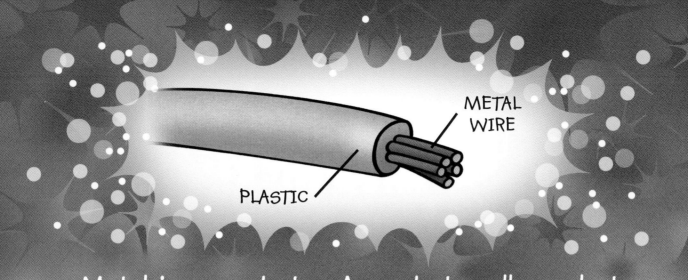

METAL WIRE

PLASTIC

Metal is a conductor. A conductor allows electrons to move through it. The metal wires are covered with plastic. Plastic is an insulator. Electrons cannot move through plastic. The plastic coating keeps the electrons from escaping, and they keep moving along the metal wires.

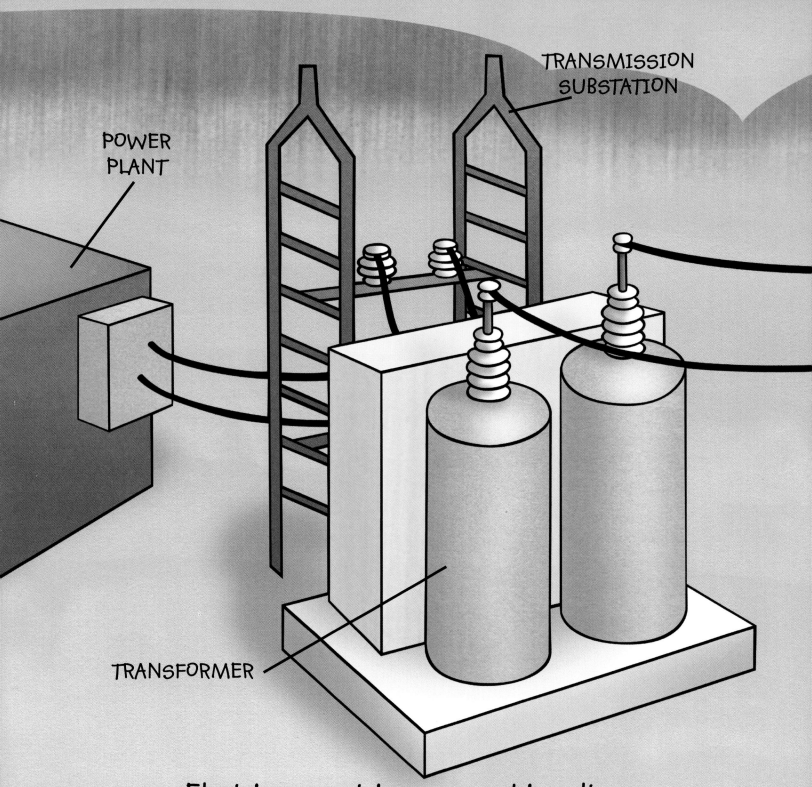

POWER
PLANT

TRANSMISSION
SUBSTATION

TRANSFORMER

Electric current is measured in voltage.
It travels from the power plant to a transformer.
The transformer increases the voltage
before it goes on its long journey.

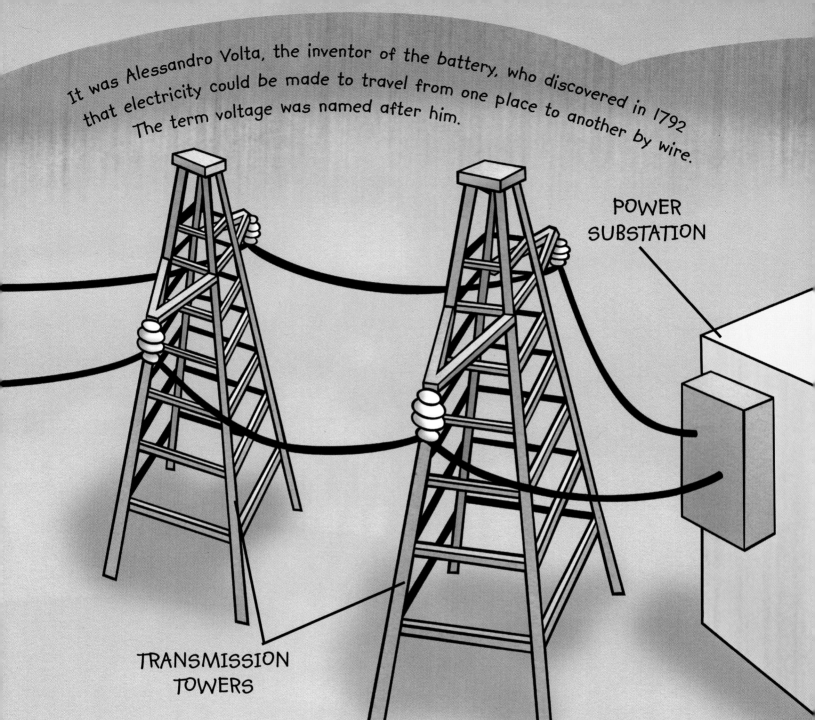

It was Alessandro Volta, the inventor of the battery, who discovered in 1792 that electricity could be made to travel from one place to another by wire. The term voltage was named after him.

POWER SUBSTATION

TRANSMISSION TOWERS

Tall towers hold the wires above the ground. They are kept out of reach because the strong current can be dangerous. When the current gets close to a town, it goes to a substation, where the voltage is lowered. That makes it safer to use.

In the town, wires carry the electric current into hospitals. The electric current runs machines that save people's lives.

The current goes to factories, too, where more machines make all kinds of things, such as sneakers, bikes, and ice cream. The electric current is sent wherever it is needed. It goes to buildings and parks, to streets and houses. It goes to your school.

At your house, wires carry electric current up through the walls. Your TV set is plugged into an outlet in the wall. Flick! You switch it on.

The current travels through
the wires to the switch.
The TV set goes on.

ELECTRIC
WIRE

When your program is over, you flick the switch off.
The current stops and the TV goes off.

One-third of the people in the world—two billion people—live without electricity. That means they have no medical equipment to help the sick, no refrigeration to keep food fresh, no electric lights for their streets and villages, and no computers or TVs.

Some people still
do not have electric power.
One day they, too, will have it,
and their lives will change.

It's time to go to sleep. You flick a switch.
The light goes out. And now you know why!

Dr. JoJo's Science Lab

Move Electrons Around

Stir Things Up

This works best indoors on a dry winter day.

1 You will need:

☐ a balloon

☐ a sweater that you're wearing, a carpet, fur, or something made of wool

2 Blow up the balloon and tie it.

3 Rub the balloon back and forth against your sweater, some fur, a carpet, or something made of wool.

4 Place the balloon against the wall and let go.

The balloon will cling to the wall. That's because you stirred up electrons all around the balloon. The static electricity is powerful enough to hold the balloon to the wall. When the electrons settle down again, the balloon will fall to the floor.

Dr. JoJo's Science Lab

Flick a Switch

Turn a Light On and Off

1 You will need:

 a working flashlight

 2 all-metal pushpins or thumbtacks

 a 4-inch length of aluminum foil from a roll

 a dry kitchen sponge or foam board about 3 inches by 6 inches

 2 metal paper clips

 a roll of tape

2

Fold the foil in half the long way and in half again. Cut off a 3 1/2 -inch strip.

3

Take the flashlight apart. Take out one of the batteries. Tape one end of the short foil strip to the flat end of the battery.

Stand the battery flat side down on the sponge. Push a pin through a paper clip, the foil strip, and the sponge.

Twist one end of the other foil strip so you can wrap it around the metal part of the flashlight *bulb* to hold it.

Pin a paper clip and the other end of the strip to the sponge. The paper clips should overlap each other about 1/2 inch.

With one hand, touch the bottom of the *bulb* to the little bump on top of the battery.

Using your other hand, move one clip over the other and press down. The *bulb* will light.

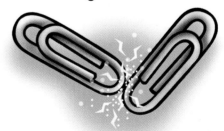

When the paper clips make contact, you let electricity from the battery flow along the metal conductor (the foil) to the bulb. When you separate the paper clips, the electricity can't go through and the light goes off.

Dr. JoJo's Science Lab

Go with the Flow

Stop and Start the Flow of Electricity

1 You will need:

 a working flashlight

 a piece of Scotch tape about 1 inch by 1 inch

 a piece of aluminum foil about 1 inch by 1 inch

2

Open the flashlight. Put the square of tape between the battery and the lightbulb. Close the flashlight and turn it on. The light will not go on.

3

Open the flashlight again. Take out the tape and put the square of aluminum foil in the same place. Close the flashlight and turn it on. The light will go on.

4

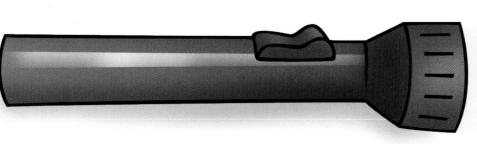

The tape is made of plastic, and plastic is an insulator, so electricity could not go from the batteries into the bulb. Aluminum is a metal, a conductor, so the electricity went through it.